SECRETS
OF AMERICAN HISTORY

MONUMENTS AND LANDMARKS

Mount Rushmore's Hidden Room and Other Monumental Secrets

by Laurie Calkhoven

illustrated by Valerio Fabbretti

Ready-to-Read

Simon Spotlight

New York   London   Toronto   Sydney   New Delhi

SIMON SPOTLIGHT
An imprint of Simon & Schuster Children's Publishing Division
1230 Avenue of the Americas, New York, New York 10020
This Simon Spotlight edition October 2018
Text copyright © 2018 by Simon & Schuster, Inc.
Illustrations copyright © 2018 by Valerio Fabbretti
All rights reserved, including the right of reproduction in whole or in part in any form.
SIMON SPOTLIGHT, READY-TO-READ, and colophon are registered trademarks of Simon & Schuster, Inc.
For information about special discounts for bulk purchases, please contact Simon & Schuster Special Sales at
1-866-506-1949 or business@simonandschuster.com.
Manufactured in the United States of America 0918 LAK
2 4 6 8 10 9 7 5 3 1
Library of Congress Cataloging-in-Publication Data 2018949723
ISBN 978-1-5344-2925-3 (hc)
ISBN 978-1-5344-2924-6 (pbk)
ISBN 978-1-5344-2926-0 (eBook)

Contents

Chapter 1: Building Boom and Bust   5

Chapter 2: The Chrysler Building's

Secret Spire   15

Chapter 3: FDR's Secret Train Station   23

Chapter 4: Mount Rushmore's Secret Room   32

But Wait . . . There's More!   42

Chapter 1
Building Boom and Bust

Did you know that many of America's landmarks and monuments came to be during a building boom in the 1920s? These skyscrapers, statues, monuments, and bridges are famous, but they also have secrets . . . some hidden, and some hiding in plain sight!

Did you know that a secret spire was hidden inside the Chrysler Building, the beautiful silver skyscraper in New York City, until the very last minute, and why? Do you know why President Franklin Delano Roosevelt had a secret train track underneath Grand Central Terminal?

There is even a secret inside Mount Rushmore, the giant monument in South Dakota carved with the faces of famous presidents! Unlock these *monumental* secrets and more—including how the Golden Gate Bridge in San Francisco got its bright orange color—in this book!

The 1920s, known as the Roaring Twenties, was a period of great change and prosperity in the United States. For the first time in history, more Americans lived in cities than on farms. Jobs were plentiful. With modern factories producing goods more quickly and cheaply than ever before, people could suddenly afford to buy things like cars, refrigerators, and pop-up toasters.

Popular culture changed too. These days you can watch television, or listen to the radio, or listen to music at home. Back then people didn't have these things in their houses. Then, in 1920, the first commercial radio station in the United States started sending news and music across the airwaves. Just three years later there were hundreds of radio stations across the country. Soon movie theaters popped up in many towns, and some people went to see a movie once a week or more.

At the same time, there was a building boom, in part because of the peace that came to the country again after World War I ended in 1918. People saw skyscrapers as symbols of progress. Advancements, like building with steel, meant that buildings could be taller than ever before.

Many of the skyscrapers and structures that people recognize today in city skylines were built during this period and the 1930s.

These include the Chrysler Building and Empire State Building in New York City, the Golden Gate Bridge and Coit Tower in San Francisco, the Hoover Dam between Arizona and Nevada, and the Coca-Cola Building in Los Angeles.

Then on October 29, 1929, a day known as "Black Tuesday," the stock market crashed. In the stock market, people try to make money by buying a small piece of a company called a "share" or a "stock," hoping to later sell it at a higher price.

When a company grows, the people who own stock in that company can make money, but when a company fails, the people can lose money. When the market crashed, many of the big investments people had made during the Roaring Twenties were suddenly worthless, almost overnight.

The crash sent the United States and the whole world into a period of hardship called the Great Depression. Banks failed, and many people lost the money they had thought was safely stored in bank accounts.

Factories closed and farmers couldn't afford to harvest their crops. Many people lost their jobs and their homes.

When Franklin Delano Roosevelt (FDR) became president of the United States in 1933, he set up a program called the New Deal to help the nation get back on track. The New Deal included free lunches for schoolchildren, a safer banking system, and the Works Progress Administration (WPA).

The WPA hired millions of people to build roads, bridges, train stations, and other structures, and to preserve national parks. While the economy eventually recovered, the buildings, monuments, and landmarks that were built during this period help tell the story of American history!

William van Alen

H. Craig Severance

Chapter 2
The Chrysler Building's
Secret Spire

During the 1920s, before the Great Depression hit, there was a building boom. Perhaps one of the most famous skyscrapers built during this time was the Chrysler Building in New York City. It all began when Walter P. Chrysler, the head of the Chrysler car company, asked an architect named William van Alen to build him the tallest building in the world.

At the same time, the Bank of the Manhattan Company hired an architect named H. Craig Severance to construct the tallest building in the world for *them* at 40 Wall Street. Van Alen and Severance had once worked together as partners, but were not on good terms anymore. They began to compete against one another . . . and used their building plans to do it!

The race was on! Month after month, people watched the Chrysler Building and the Bank of the Manhattan Company building rise higher and higher. The architects kept changing their plans to keep up with each other. Some say that at first the 40 Wall Street building was going to be just forty-seven stories, but the architect kept adding floors to keep up with the Chrysler Building!

It seemed like the Bank of the Manhattan

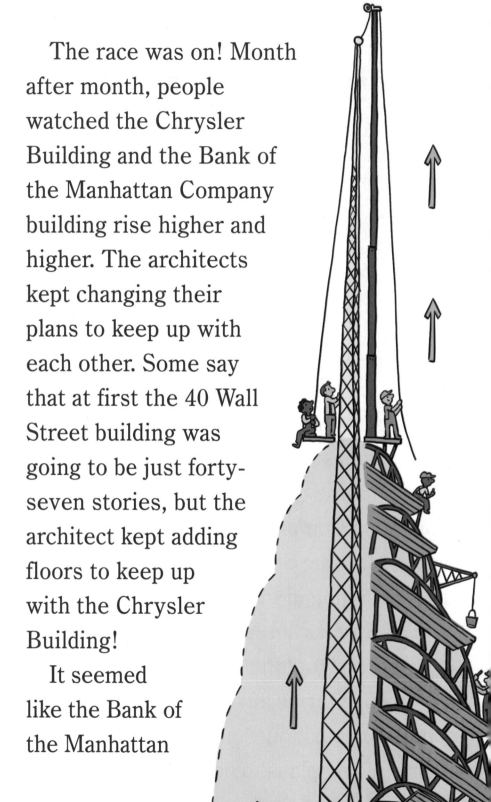

Company building was going to win. When it was finished in the fall of 1929, it had a fifty-foot-tall flagpole on top that gave it an extra boost. People assumed that at 927 feet tall and seventy-one stories, it had won the race. But had it?

Van Alen had a secret plan for how to win the title of tallest building. He was constructing a spire inside his tower and hiding it until right before the Chrysler Building would open, to keep anyone from finding out how tall it would really be.

In October 1929 the secret spire was pushed up through the top of the building's tower. The seventy-seven-story building was now 1,046 feet tall—119 feet taller than its downtown rival! Van Alen and his Chrysler Building had won! It was the tallest building in the world . . . for nearly a year.

Even better than winning was the fact that the Chrysler Building was celebrated for its beauty, and became a landmark. From the sunburst pattern on its crown to its stainless steel gargoyles (GAR-goils) shaped like eagles—and like the shiny eagle metal hood decorations on Chrysler cars—the Chrysler Building is still one of the most photographed buildings in the world.

William van Alen was so proud of his achievement that he dressed up as the Chrysler Building for an architects' ball in 1931!

But soon a new skyscraper would tower above all the rest—the Empire State Building. The plan was for it to be 1,050 feet tall. Then the builder realized that was just four feet taller than the Chrysler Building and decided to add a "crown" or a "hat" decoration to the top, to be safe (more on that later). That brought the Empire State Building to a height of 1,250 feet when it opened in May 1931. (A 204-foot-tall antenna was added years later.) It became the tallest building in the world, and held on to that title until 1970, when the North Tower of the World Trade Center became the tallest building in the world while still under construction.

In the worst days of the Great Depression, New Yorkers watched this new skyscraper rise. Newspaper reporters called this building boom "The Race into the Sky." It was a symbol of hope in one of our country's darkest times.

Chapter 3
FDR's Secret Train Station

Franklin Delano Roosevelt was inaugurated, or sworn in, as president of the United States on March 4, 1933, in the middle of the Great Depression. In his inauguration speech he said, "The only thing we have to fear is fear itself," and he promised to work for better times ahead.

President Roosevelt knew that the American people needed a strong leader to see them through the tough times. So he kept a very big secret from them: In 1921 the then thirty-nine-year-old FDR came down with a disease that left him unable to walk. His condition was most likely caused by a disease called polio, but historians are not certain.

We now have a vaccine (vak-SEEN) for polio that can keep people from getting sick, but it hadn't been invented yet when FDR fell ill. Polio makes people's muscles weak. Many people got better, but others were left paralyzed (PARE-uh-lized) and unable to walk, or only with great difficulty.

FDR was unable to move from the waist down. He spent most of his time in a wheelchair.

We know better now, but back then many people didn't believe a person with different abilities could be president. FDR didn't think the American people would have confidence in him if they knew the truth. So he and his staff came up with creative ways to hide his secret. They made sure that he was always seen standing upright in public.

He sometimes used special braces on  his legs, and crutches to prop himself up, or supported himself during speeches by leaning on a stand called a lectern that was bolted to the floor. He was almost never seen getting in and out of cars, and he found ways to avoid being seen in his wheelchair.

One of them was a top secret train station hidden underground in New York City! The platform, an extension of Grand Central Terminal, was underneath the famous Waldorf Astoria Hotel. FDR had to travel to New York often when he was president. No one ever saw him being wheeled on or off the train because of the secret platform!

It wasn't just FDR's platform that was special. So was the president's train. The train's last car was built to hold the president's limousine. When they arrived at the Waldorf, a door on the side of the last train car opened up, and FDR's driver could drive right off the train and onto a special elevator that brought them to the hotel.

Rumor has it that even today the station is available whenever a president is in New York City—in case of emergency—but the people who might know the truth aren't telling!

What do you think?

Grand Central Secrets

In addition to its hush-hush presidential tunnels and platform, Grand Central Terminal has other secrets. Over the years those secrets have included a hidden apartment and two tennis courts. Tennis stars Venus and Serena Williams even played there!

The station's *most expensive* little-known fact might have to do with the clock on top of the information booth. The clock face is made from opal—a precious gem—that is worth as much as twenty million dollars!

That might be the shiniest secret, but the biggest secret related to Grand Central Terminal is still FDR's train platform!

Chapter 4
Mount Rushmore's Secret Room

You've probably heard of the Mount Rushmore National Memorial—the giant monument of four presidential faces carved into the side of a mountain in the Black Hills of South Dakota. But did you know that the sixty-foot-tall heads of George Washington, Thomas Jefferson, Theodore Roosevelt, and Abraham Lincoln are hiding something surprising?

First, a little history: The idea for the monument came from a South Dakota state historian named Doane Robinson who wanted to build something to bring tourists to the state. While that part of his plan was a success and Mount Rushmore became a cherished landmark for many people, it came at a very high price. It is important to know about and respect the history, even though it is an unhappy one:

Mount Rushmore is carved out of land that belonged to American Indians from the Sioux tribes, who had lived there for thousands of years before the United States existed. They called the mountain "The Six Grandfathers" and were promised the rights to their land in 1868, in the Treaty of Fort Laramie. Then gold was discovered in the Black Hills, and the Sioux were forced to leave against their will. This area and the monument itself are still involved in a legal battle. To make matters worse, the name of the mountain was changed to "Mount Rushmore" after a lawyer named Charles Rushmore traveled there.

When sculptor Gutzon Borglum was hired to create the monument, he chose the presidents he believed had had the greatest impact on the United States at that point in time.

Work began in 1927. During the next fourteen years, nearly four hundred workers climbed up hundreds of steps to get to the work site every day! But Borglum was afraid that as years and centuries passed, people might forget why those faces were carved into a mountain. His first solution to that problem was to plan for a large plaque on the mountain that would describe the most important events in American history. But there was no way to make the words big enough so that people could read them from the ground!

So Borglum came up with another
plan . . . and this is where the secret comes
in! Just behind Lincoln's head is an unfinished
room that Borglum built *inside* the mountain.
He wanted Mount Rushmore to shine a
light on democracy. He built the room as a
"Hall of Records" to include a history of the
carvings on Mount Rushmore and copies of
the nation's most important documents. He
planned for an eight-hundred-foot stairway to
lead to an eighty-by-one-hundred-foot room.

In 1938, while work continued on the faces, Borglum created an opening right in the stone behind Lincoln's head to begin work on his hall.

Soon after, the government told the sculptor to forget about the room and focus on finishing the presidents. The original plan was actually for the monument to show the presidents from the waist up!

Then Borglum died in March 1941, and his son, Lincoln, took over, but the workers were ordered to stop carving when the presidents' faces were finished. World War II had begun, and the United States needed to save money in case they decided to join the battle.

Finally, on October 31, 1941, the Mount Rushmore National Memorial was declared completed—without the Hall of Records and without the torsos of the presidents.

Borglum's family never gave up on his idea for a Hall of Records. They created carved panels to tell the story of the sculptor, his presidential subjects, and how the carving on the mountain had been made. Other panels were inscribed with the words of the Declaration of Independence, the Bill of Rights, and other precious American documents.

On August 9, 1998, four generations of the sculptor's family gathered in the small, unfinished room Borglum had built. The panels were placed inside a teakwood box that was then put into a titanium vault. Centuries from now, according to Borglum's dream, even if civilization as we know it no longer exists, anyone who finds the mountain and its secret room will learn about the United States and democracy from those documents.

Many plans were changed during the boom and bust years in the United States, but in the end, the country became stronger thanks to the dedication of the people—many whose names are long forgotten—who worked behind the scenes to make the country's monuments, buildings, and landmarks!

Read on to learn more about the secrets of American history, including surprising stories about monuments and landmarks from around the country, the symbols behind the Statue of Liberty, and more!

More Monumental Secrets!

There are surprises in landmarks and monuments all over the United States. Here are more to discover:

Empire State Building

When the Empire State Building was nearly finished, the construction chairman and former New York governor  Al Smith had the idea to add a "crown" in the form of a two-hundred-foot spire where airships could dock. Airships, also called blimps or dirigibles (DEER-ih-jih-buls), are a bit like balloons. They are filled with gas that is lighter than air, such as helium, which allows them to float or fly.

The spire made the building the tallest in the world . . . but winds at that height made the plan for airships impossible.

The building still has a staircase in the spire for that purpose, and a secret 102nd floor that was meant to be a waiting room for airship passengers! It is now off-limits to the public, but sometimes public figures get to visit it. Can you imagine if giant airships were anchored in the sky at the top of the Empire State Building?

The Golden Gate Bridge

The bridge, which opened in 1937, wasn't supposed to be the orange color we've all come to know and love. The US Navy, worried that ships wouldn't see the bridge in foggy conditions, wanted it painted in black and yellow stripes. The Army Air Corps thought red and white stripes would make the bridge more visible from the air.

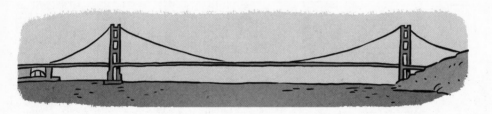

The orange color was just a primer, or base coat of paint, to protect the steel from the elements (like salt water) before the bridge's actual paint color was applied. But the bridge's architect, Irving Morrow, liked the orange color and decided to keep it because he thought it blended in with the hills around San Francisco. Now it is hard to imagine the Golden Gate Bridge as anything other than its iconic golden orange!

Gateway Arch, St. Louis

St. Louis's famous Gateway Arch was designed to symbolize Thomas Jefferson's vision of a United States that expanded from Atlantic to Pacific. It also celebrates St. Louis's role in the country's westward expansion.

At 630 feet tall, it's the tallest man-made monument in the United States. The monument was completed in 1965, and trams have been carrying visitors to the top since 1967. Before it was finished, a time capsule holding the signatures of more than 700,000 local residents—mostly schoolchildren—was sealed inside! Students enrolled in public schools were asked to participate. It was put inside the keystone, a stone that is placed at the top of arches to help them hold their shape. Even if the time capsule is never opened, people whose signatures are inside will always know that they were a part of history!

Secrets of the Statue of Liberty

The Statue of Liberty was a gift from the people of France to the people of the United States and was finished in 1886. It was designed by a sculptor named Frédéric-Auguste Bartholdi and the engineer Alexandre-Gustave Eiffel, who is best known for designing the Eiffel Tower in Paris, France.

The Statue of Liberty was built on the site of an old fort, called Fort Wood, which was in the shape of an eleven-sided star. The fort was built on an island called Bedloe Island, which is now called Liberty Island.

Did you know that there's a secret room inside the Statue of Liberty's torch? At first it was open to the public. Then, on July 30, 1916, during World War I, German spies caused an explosion on Black Tom Island, which is near Liberty Island. The blast was felt as far away as Times Square in Manhattan and damaged the Statue of Liberty's torch. The room has been off-limits ever since!

Symbols

You might already know about the symbolism of the Statue of Liberty's torch, which is said to light the way for immigrants looking to find freedom, safety, and happiness in America, but there are more symbols in the statue.

• The seven rays of her crown are meant to look like rays of sunshine.

• She stands in the middle of broken chains and her right foot is raised. This symbolizes the struggle to be free, as if she were breaking out of her chains. Some say it represents how the American colonies broke free of British rule to form the United States, but the original intention was for it to represent the end of all types of slavery.

Fun Facts about Lady Liberty

• She has very big feet: Her shoe size is 879!

• She is hit by more than six hundred bolts of lightning every year!

• She was originally called "Liberty Enlightening the World."

TAKE THE MOUNT RUSHMORE'S HIDDEN ROOM AND OTHER MONUMENTAL SECRETS QUIZ

1. What is another name for the 1920s in America?

a. Building Twenties   b. Roaring Twenties   c. Yelling Twenties

2. In what year did the stock market crash, setting off the Great Depression?

a. 1919   b. 1939   c. 1929

3. In what state is Mount Rushmore?

a. South Dakota   b. North Dakota   c. South Carolina

4. What disease or illness may have caused President Franklin Delano Roosevelt to lose the ability to walk?

a. polio   b. influenza   c. chicken pox

5. What was added to the top of the Chrysler Building to make it even taller?

a. a spire   b. a radio antenna   c. a nest

6. What pattern did some people want to be painted on the Golden Gate Bridge?

a. hearts   b. dots   c. stripes

7. Behind which president's head is the door to the hidden room at Mount Rushmore?

a. Taft   b. Lincoln   c. Obama

8. The gargoyles at the top of the Chrysler Building are in the shape of what animal?

a. eagles   b. cats   c. fish

Answers: 1.b 2.c 3.a 4.a 5.a 6.c 7.b 8.a